One, two

One, two, three, four, five,
Once I caught a fish alive!
Six, seven, eight, nine, ten,
Then I let it go again!
Why did you let it go?
Because it bit my finger so.
Which finger did it bite?
This little finger on the right.

Five little astronauts

One little astronaut
Feeling rather blue,
Asked her friend to come and play –
One and one makes two.

Two little astronauts
Sitting down to tea,
Asked their friend to come and eat –
Two and one makes three.

Three little astronauts
Knocking at the door,
Asked their friend to come and stay –
Three and one makes four.

Four little astronauts
Going for a drive,
Asked their friend to come along –
Four and one makes five.

Five little astronauts
Aiming for the moon
Getting ready, getting set –
They'll blast off very soon!

5-4-3-2-1-BLAST OFF!

5-4-3-2-1 Blast Off!

Hippety hop

Hippety hop to the bakers shop
To buy three sticks of candy
One for you, one for me and one for sister Sandy.

Hippety hop to the bakers shop
To buy four sticks of candy
One for you, one for me and two for sister Sandy.

Hippety hop to the bakers shop
To buy five sticks of candy
One for you, one for me and three for sister Sandy.

Rockets

Rockets shoot off into space,
Hurry up it's quite a race.
Rockets make a big loud boom,
Heading up towards the moon,
Counting down before we go,
10, 9, 8, 7, 6, 5, 4, 3, 2, 1, ZERO!

Playing opposites

If I say big,
Will you say small?
If I say short,
Will you say tall?

If I say fast,
Will you say slow?
If I say high,
Will you say low?

If I say left,
Will you say right?
If I say day,
Will you say night?

Seven dizzy dragons

Seven dizzy dragons spinning round and round,
One falls and bumps its head and tumbles to the ground.

Six dizzy dragons spinning round and round,
One falls and bumps its head and tumbles to the ground.

Five dizzy dragons spinning round and round,
One falls and bumps its head and tumbles to the ground.

Four dizzy dragons spinning round and round,
One falls and bumps its head and tumbles to the ground.

Three dizzy dragons spinning round and round,
One falls and bumps its head and tumbles to the ground.

Two dizzy dragons spinning round and round,
One falls and bumps its head and tumbles to the ground.

One dizzy dragon spinning round and round,
It falls and bumps its head and tumbles to the ground.

No dizzy dragons spinning round and round
they all jump up and creep away without a single sound.

Ten little teddies

Ten little teddies walking in a line,
One chased a golden cloud, and then there were nine.

Nine little teddies learning how to skate,
One skated out of sight, and then there were eight.

Eight little teddies, going down to Devon,
One stopped to have some tea, and then there were seven.

Seven little teddies, playing lots of tricks,
One waved her magic wand, and then there were six.

Six little teddies, learning how to dive,
One landed far away, so then there were five.

Five little teddies, sliding on the floor,
One slid right past the rest, and then there were four.

Four little teddies, sailing out to sea,
One chased a mermaid and then there were three.

Three little teddies, finding things to do,
One learnt to fly away, and then there were two.

Two little teddies, having lots of fun,
One went on holiday, so then there was one.

One little teddy, lonely in the sun,
She went to find her friends, so then there were none.

Imaginary pictures

Draw a circle in the air.
Start from here and go to where'?
Pretend your finger is the pen,
Draw round and round and back again.

Draw a square above your head,
Or draw it by your feet instead.
One side, two sides, three and four.
Why not try to draw some more?

Draw a triangle in the sky.
Is it short or is it high?
Corners where you turn your pen,
One, two, three, then start again.

Think what all our shapes could be,
Plates, a box, a Christmas tree,
Rocket, lorry, bat or ball,
Shapes can help you draw them all.

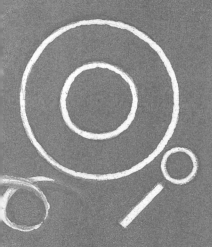

9

Patterns

I can make a pattern
You can make it too.
I'll start mine with splish splosh,
Now it's up to you.
Splish splosh splish splosh . . .

I can make a pattern
You can make it too.
I'll start mine with 1, 2,
Now it's up to you.
1, 2, 3, 1, 2, 3, . . .

I can make a pattern
You can make it too
I'll start mine with red, blue,
Now it's up to you.
red, blue, red, blue, red, blue,

I can make a pattern
You can make it too
I'll start mine with left, right,
Now it's up to you.
left, right, left, right, left, right,

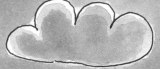
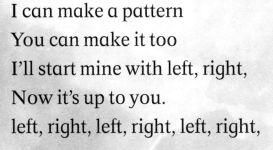

Noah's ark traditional

1 Now in came the animals two by two,
   The hippo and the kangaroo.

Chorus Who built the Ark?
        Noah! Noah!
        Who built the Ark?
        Brother Noah built the Ark.

2 Now in came the animals four by four,
   Two through the window and two through the door.

3 Now in came the animals six by six,
   The elephants laughed at the monkeys' tricks.

4 Now in came the animals eight by eight,
   Some were on time and some were late.

5 Now in came the animals ten by ten,
   Five black roosters and five black hens.

6 Now Noah said: 'Go SHUT THAT DOOR!
   The rain is falling, we can't take more.'

The chimpanzees' tea party

Ten hungry chimpanzees
Gather round to feed.
Each wants one cherry cake –
That's ten small cakes we'll need.

Ten hungry chimpanzees
Gather round to feed.
Each wants two sausage rolls –
That's twenty rolls we'll need!

Ten hungry chimpanzees
Gather round to feed.
Each wants three purple plums –
That's thirty plums we'll need.

Ten hungry chimpanzees
Gather round to feed.
Each wants four chunks of cheese –
That's forty chunks we'll need.

Ten hungry chimpanzees
Gather round to feed.
Each wants five chocolate bars –
That's fifty bars we'll need.

Ten hungry chimpanzees
Gather round to feed.
Each wants six purple grapes –
That's sixty grapes we'll need.

Ten hungry chimpanzees
Gather round to feed.
Each wants seven crunchy crisps –
That's seventy crisps we'll need.

Ten hungry chimpanzees
Gather round to feed.
Each wants eight bags of nuts –
That's eighty bags we'll need.

Ten hungry chimpanzees
Gather round to feed.
Each wants nine apple pies –
That's ninety pies we'll need.

Ten hungry chimpanzees
Gather round to feed.
Each wants ten honey bars –
A hundred bars we'll need.

Ten chubby chimpanzees
Gather round to feed,
Couldn't eat another bite,
There's nothing's more we need.

The big red bus

Along comes the big red bus
Ten children at the stop
Ten children go downstairs
None climb to the top.

Along comes the big red bus
Ten children at the stop
Nine children go downstairs
One climbs to the top.

Along comes the big red bus
Ten children at the stop
Eight children go downstairs
Two climb to the top.

Along comes the big red bus
Ten children at the stop
Seven children go downstairs
Three climb to the top.

Along comes the big red bus
Ten children at the stop
Six children go downstairs
Four climb to the top.

Along comes the big red bus
Ten children at the stop
Five children go downstairs
Five climb to the top.

Twelve red balloons

Twelve red balloons hanging from a tree
Woosh blows the wind
And two fly free.

Ten red balloons hanging from a tree
Woosh blows the wind
And two fly free.

Eight red balloons hanging from a tree
Woosh blows the wind
And two fly free.

Six red balloons hanging from a tree
Woosh blows the wind
And two fly free.

Four red balloons hanging from a tree
Woosh blows the wind
And two fly free.

Two red balloons hanging from a tree
Woosh blows the wind
And both fly free.

No red balloons hanging from a tree
Woosh blows the wind
But they've all flown free!

The happy clowns

Ten happy clowns
Were standing in a row.
The first said 'Good-day!'
And the second bowed low.
The third clapped his hands,
And the fourth turned around,
The fifth stamped his feet,
And the sixth touched the ground.
The seventh gave a hop,
The eighth jumped so high.
The ninth gave a wave,
And the tenth said 'Good-bye!'

Anna had a cart

Anna had a cart
and she had fun
selling oranges
in the sun
1 on Monday
2 on Tuesday
3 on Wednesday
4 on Thursday
5 on Friday
6 on Saturday
7 on Sunday
Can you count them?
Can you tell?
How many oranges
did she sell?

M T W Th F S Su

What's the time, Mr Wolf?

Early one morning
Red Riding Hood said:
What's the time, Mr Wolf?
And he scratched his big head.

Nine o'clock – it's early
And I'm still in bed!

One whole hour later
Red Riding Hood said:
What's the time, Mr Wolf?
And he scratched his big head.

Ten o'clock – it's later
But I'm still in bed!

One whole hour later
Red Riding Hood said:
What's the time, Mr Wolf?
And he scratched his big head.

Eleven o'clock – it's later
But I'm still in bed!

One whole hour later
Red Riding Hood said:
What's the time, Mr Wolf?
And he scratched his big head.

Twelve o'clock – it's lunchtime
And it's time I was fed!

Swing your arms

To the left
To the right
Touch your knees
Then your toes,

To the left
To the right
Touch your shoulders
Then your nose.

To the left
To the right
Reach up high
Touch the ground,

To the left
To the right
Spin yourself
A whole turn round

19

How much change?

Customer: Shopkeeper, please
Will you sell me some tea?

Shopkeeper: A packet costs six pence.
Customer: I'll give you 10p.

Customer: Shopkeeper, please
How much change will there be?

Shopkeeper: Six pence from ten pence …

Customer: That's four pence for me!

Shoemaker, shoemaker

Shoemaker, shoemaker,
make me some shoes.
I don't have any to wear.
How many feet do you have, little Ted?
Why, two, can't you see them down there?

Shoemaker, shoemaker,
make me some shoes.
I don't have any to wear.
How many feet do you have, little horse?
Why, four, can't you see them down there?

Shoemaker, shoemaker,
make me some shoes.
I don't have any to wear.
How many feet do you have, little ant?
Why, six, can't you see them down there?

Shoemaker, shoemaker,
make me some shoes.
I don't have any to wear.
How many feet do you have, spider dear?
Why, eight, can't you see them down there?

Shoemaker, shoemaker,
make me some shoes.
I don't have any to wear.
How many feet do you have, monster dear?
Why, ten, can't you see them down there?

How many shoes would our shoemaker need
to fit every bare-footed friend?
Can you add two and four, then six, eight and ten
That's the number he makes by the end.

Lily pads

One spotted frog, stretching out his toe,
Ten flat lily leaves all in a row,
Start at leaf number one,
Hop in twos till you're done,
Odd numbers in a line,
One, three, five, seven, nine.

One spotted frog, stretching out his toe,
Ten flat lily leaves all in a row,
Start at leaf number two,
Hop two leaves, till you're through,
Even numbers you have then,
Two, four, six, eight, ten.

Chook, chook

Chook, chook, chook-chook-chook
Good morning Mrs Hen
How many chickens have you got?
Madam I've got ten.
Four of them are yellow
and four of them are brown
and two of them are speckled red
The nicest in the town.

Number patterns

I can count way up high
count up in steps of 2
2, 4, 6, 8, ...

I can count way up high,
count up in steps of 3
3, 6, 9, ...

I can count way up high,
count up in steps of 4
4, 8, 12, ...

I can count way up high,
count up in steps of 5
5, 10, 15, 20, ...

Twenty slithery slippery snakes

Twenty slithery slippery snakes
Tried to make some chocolate cakes,
Five preferred to read a book
Leaving 15 home to cook.

Fifteen slithery, slippery snakes,
Tried to make some chocolate cakes
Five preferred to read a book
Leaving 10 at home to cook.

Ten slithery slippery snakes
Tried to make some chocolate cakes,
Five preferred to read a book
Leaving 5 at home to cook.

Five slithery slippery snakes
Tried to make some chocolate cakes,
Five preferred to read a book
Leaving none at home to cook.

Maybe I can count the stars

Maybe I can count the stars
That twinkle in the sky so bright.
Are there hundreds, thousands, millions
Winking at me in the night?

Ten and ten and ten more there –
But doing this will take all night!
Maybe there are millions, billions,
Are there more still out of sight?

Twelve little monkeys

Twelve little monkeys
Getting in a fix,
Half ran away
And then there were six.

Ten very busy bees
Looking for a hive,
Half flew away
And then there were five.

Eight fluffy kittens
Scratching at the door
Half bounced away
And then there were four.

Six pretty parrots
Flying wild and free,
Half flew away
So then there were three.

Four furry fieldmice
Playing in the dew
Half ran away
So then there were two!

Two huge crocodiles
Basking in the sun,
Half swam away
So then there was one.

Birthday cake

How shall we share our birthday cake?
How shall we share our birthday cake?
A quarter for you,
A quarter for me,
A quarter for Mina
And a quarter for Bea.

How shall we share our birthday cake?
How shall we share our birthday cake?
A half for you
A half for me,
Then none for Mina
And none for Bea!

A square dance

Step forward one,
Little robot,
Clap your hands one two three!
Turn to your right,
Little robot,
And tap tap tap each knee.

Step forward one,
Little robot,
Clap your hands one two three!
Turn to your right,
Little robot,
And tap tap tap each knee.

Step forward one,
Little robot,
Clap your hands one two three!
Turn to your right,
Little robot,
You're home again you see!

Step forward one,
Little robot,
Clap your hands one two three!
Turn to your right,
Little robot,
And tap tap tap each knee.

Circle of seasons

Spring is early in the year,
Spring, summer, autumn, winter,
Summer follows, sunshine's here,
Spring, summer, autumn, winter,
Autumn next as leaves turn brown,
Spring, summer, autumn, winter,
Winter's last, the snow falls down,
Spring, summer, autumn, winter,
As winter ends another year,
Spring, summer, autumn, winter,
Start again for spring is here,
Spring, summer, autumn, winter.

Notes

p4 Hippety hop: Vary this by using any numbers you like. How many rhymes can you make using the same number of sticks of candy?

p6 Playing opposites: This can be done to appropriate actions using just arms and hands. For fast and slow, children can run one hand up an arm, pretending it is a rabbit or a snail. You can also develop ideas of other opposites when talking to the children, such as wide and narrow, day and night, hello and good-bye, summer and winter.

p10 Patterns: These patterns are all repeating patterns. You could vary this and use growing patterns, eg 1, 2, 3, ... (or 2, 4, 6, ...) in line three, and then 1, 2, 3, 4, 5, 6, (or 2, 4, 6, 8, 10) in the last line.

p15 Twelve red balloons: You can ask twelve children to stand up to be the balloons. They can sit down when they are blown away. You could also start from ten, twenty etc.

p16 The happy clowns: A group of ten children can be chosen to stand where everyone can see them, and do the actions.

p17 Anna had a cart: You could start with just two or three days, and build up to the whole rhyme. (music below)

p18 What's the time Mr Wolf? Half the class could be Red Riding Hood and the other half the wolf. You can vary the starting time and the interval, eg start at eight o'clock and use 'two hours later'.

p19 Swing your arms. (music below)

p20 How much change?: (Individuals should suggest ways of making up the change:

2p and 2p make four pence
1p and 1p and 2p makes four pence.

Different groups or individuals can take the part of the shopkeeper and customer. Vary the amounts of money as appropriate for the children, eg

Customer: Shopkeeper, please
          Will you sell me some tea?
Shopkeeper: A packet costs thirty pence.
Customer: I'll give you 50p.

Anna had a cart

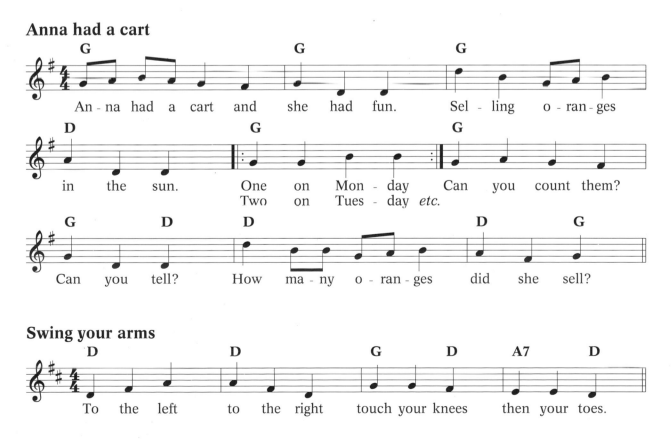

Swing your arms

p23 Chook, Chook: You could change the numbers of the yellow, brown and speckled red eggs so that you are exploring number bonds of ten. You could have a different number of chicks. So you could finish:

Madam I've got eight
One of them is yellow and three of them are brown
and four of them are speckled red
the nicest in the town.

p25 Twenty slithery slippery snakes: You could start with much larger numbers according to the experiences of your children. You could go back in tens as in the example below, or you might need to go back in fifties. Let children choose a starting number – expect them to say a thousand or a million!)
100 slither slippery snakes
Tried to make some chocolate cake
10 preferred to read a book
Leaving 90 at home to cook.

p26 Maybe I can count the stars: The stars are grouped in tens to make counting easier. Encourage children to try to count them when they are reading the book with a friend. The rhyme is intended to promote discussion about large numbers and can be used alongside other place value or calculator work in which children explore large numbers.

p28 Birthday cake:
Children could make up their own variations. For example:

How shall we share our birthday cake?
How shall we share our birthday cake?
A half for you
A quarter for me,
A quarter for Mina
But none for Bea!

How shall we share our birthday cake?
How shall we share our birthday cake?
A quarter for me
Three quarters for you!
But none for Sally
And none for Sue!

p29 A square dance: Vary this using 'left' instead of 'right', 'step forward two/three' etc. 'Can you make a rectangle?'(music below)

p30 Circle of Seasons: The teacher could read lines 1, 3, 5, etc and the children could chant the refrain. Older children could learn lines 1, 3, 5, etc first as a poem, then add the repeating line later. It could be a skipping rhyme. Two children turn the rope whilst others run in or out. Children decide on a season and can only join or leave the skipping on that word.

A square dance

Step forward one little robot. Clap your hands one two three

Turn to your right little robot. And tap tap tap each knee.